small lives

ALSO BY gary jackson

Missing You, Metropolis

origin story: poems

The **MARY BURRITT CHRISTIANSEN POETRY SERIES** publishes two to four books a year that engage and give voice to the realities of living, working, and experiencing the West and the Border as places and as metaphors. The purpose of the series is to expand access to, and the audience for, quality poetry, both single volumes and anthologies, that can be used for general reading as well as in classrooms.

Also available in the **MARY BURRITT CHRISTIANSEN POETRY SERIES**:

a chronology of blood: poems by Teo Shannon
A Real Man Would Have a Gun: Poems by Stacey Waite
Dream of the Bird Tattoo: Poems and Sueñitos by Juan J. Morales
Unruly Tree: Poems by Leslie Ullman
A Walk with Frank O'Hara: Poems by Susan Aizenberg
Light of Wings: Poems by Sarah Kotchian
Trials and Tribulations of Dirty Shame, Oklahoma: And Other Prose Poems by Sy Hoahwah
A Guide to Tongue Tie Surgery: Poems by Tina Carlson
Point of Entry: Poems by Katherine DiBella Seluja
Suggest Paradise: Poems by Ray Gonzalez

For additional titles in the **MARY BURRITT CHRISTIANSEN POETRY SERIES**, please visit unmpress.com.

Mary Burritt Christiansen Poetry Series

HILDA RAZ, Series Editor

small lives

poems

gary jackson

UNIVERSITY OF NEW MEXICO PRESS

ALBUQUERQUE

© 2025 by Gary Jackson
All rights reserved. Published 2025
Printed in the United States of America

ISBN 978-0-8263-6842-3 (paper)
ISBN 978-0-8263-6843-0 (electronic)

Library of Congress Control Number: 2025932503

Founded in 1889, the University of New Mexico sits on the traditional homelands of the Pueblo of Sandia. The original peoples of New Mexico—Pueblo, Navajo, and Apache—since time immemorial have deep connections to the land and have made significant contributions to the broader community statewide. We honor the land itself and those who remain stewards of this land throughout the generations and also acknowledge our committed relationship to Indigenous peoples. We gratefully recognize our history.

Cover illustration by Isaac Morris
Cover images adapted from photos courtesy of Piere Bamin, Jack Van Hel, Evie Shaffer, and NASA.
Designed by Isaac Morris
Composed in Adobe Jenson Pro and Vendetta

for you

> Whole countries hover, oblivious on the edge / of history
> —LYNDA HULL

> but not you, not with / metropolis to save
> —LUCILLE CLIFTON

Contents

comic book plots & origin stories — 1

Dramatis Personae — 2

I

fiat lux — 5

The Invincible Woman introduces herself — 6

The Willpower Man says danger — 7

The Telepath — 8

on visibility — 9

The Invincible Woman makes the front page — 10

The Precog — 11

The Invincible Woman goes to a party — 13

on restorative justice and Tony Danza — 14

rule of gravity — 15

rehearsal — 16

The Telepath follows the bad man — 17

The Invincible Woman enjoys her night off — 18

The Telepath tries you on — 19

tales to astonish — 20

meanwhile… — 22

    a   A   a — 23

The Telepath tells your fortune — 24

men on fire — 25

The Telepath turned broken record — 26

our leader — 27

respite — 28

▓▓▓▓▓▓▓▓ History Month — 34

on the clock — 35

no more water — 36

stranger things — 37

on language — 38

a different world — 39

old lions — 40

the golden age — 42

II

promotion — 45

tryouts — 46

Welcome to The Amazing, Invincible Woman! Hope you survive the experience! — 47

The Telepath discovers a new gift — 48

on acceptance — 49

on power — 50

The Amazing — 51

The Telepath consoles The Willpower Man — 52

The Invincible Woman has a case of the Mondays — 53

birthday cake — 54

on sorrow & joy — 55

next — 56

in blackest day, in brightest night — 57

The Telepath quits her day job — 58

assembly — 59

The Telepath listens to the flowers and trees — 60

new gods — 61

The Telepath attends a book club — 62

exhibition — 63

Astro Boy blues — 64

Beast Boy — 65

on vulnerability — 67

The Telepath finds the bright side — 68

population boom — 69

III

the new rules — 73

early retirement — 74

The Willpower Man — 79

The Invincible Woman
goes viral — 80

Doctor Freeman — 81

you're watching tv in your
own home — 82

the handcuffs — 83

The Invincible Woman reunites
with The Telepath — 85

The Invincible Woman
learns to fly — 87

newscast — 88

The Invincible Woman and
The Willpower Man make
a comeback — 89

acts of kindness — 90

The Invincible Woman
attends a meeting — 91

The Never-Ending Man — 92

The Invincible Girl — 94

move — 95

Goliath — 96

moon — 99

necropolis — 104

The Heartless Boy — 106

IV

The Invincible Woman
becomes god — 109

Epilogue

small lives — 121
Bruce's Beach — 122
overdue — 123
origin story — 124
The Invincible Woman has a one-night stand — 125

on corrective thinking — 126
osteology — 127
fly — 130
the new world — 131
work — 132

Acknowledgements — 135

Notes — 137

small lives

comic book plots & origin stories

He believes he's a brand-new thing. *I can change the world*, he says, which is true. But we're all such small things compared to the history beneath us, and yet history is all we see. In not-so-polite terms, he asks us to move out of his way. We refuse. We push him into the earth. He gets back up, then demands to know *what made you so special?* We ignore the past tense, as if we're no longer who we are. We take turns: I was sold, she was adopted, you were orphaned, all of us raised by a system that taught us how to be what we did not want to be but are. Weapons to be used, stars to be touched, animals to be brought low. Fearsome things. Built to withstand the country that built us. *Why can't I, too, walk in light?* He clenches his fists. It's cruel, what happens next.

Dramatis Personae

Usually / but not always:

>The Invincible Woman / you
>The Telepath / she
>The Willpower Man / I

>we / us / them

There are, of course, countless others.

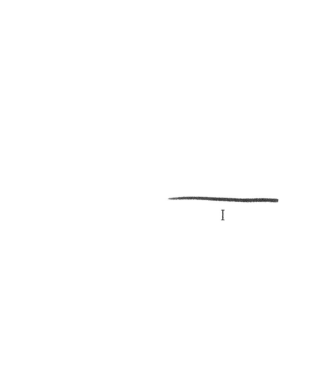

I

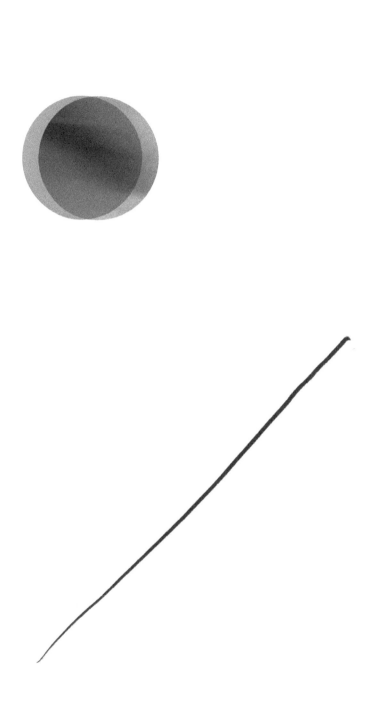

fiat lux

> The first moon will be mostly experimental, but the three moons in 2022 will be the real deal, with great civic and commercial potential.
>
> —Wu Chunfeng, chairman of Chengdu Aerospace Science and Technology Microelectronics System Research Institute

Imagine the moon times two, times four, times several times more until there's a moon for every country: all that wonderful moonlight filling parking lots and lonely street corners, and how we'll love it at first and wonder what, exactly, powers each moon, and how did we secure all the moons in place? When we look up, how many lights are stars, or just us staring back? We give them names: Luna Lovegood, Beyoncé, Doris Day. We know it's pointless: finding faces in our newborn lunar bodies: craterless and vast, snow white and smooth: our new favorite things.

The Invincible Woman introduces herself

You knock on the killers' door. When they answer, they see you alone with a name tag, a handful of pamphlets, and questions about renewable energy and have they ever considered solar panels? They're guarded at first, but when you ask if you could have a drink of water, they invite you inside where the air conditioner is cranked so low you can see your breath and the sofa is covered in plastic like your grandmama's house, though everything smells like Lysol and day-old coffee. You push on—ask to use the bathroom and if you were a man, you doubt you would've gotten this far, but they don't see you as a threat, not until a young man catches you snooping in a bedroom, looking under the bed for a trap door or some clue that will lead you towards the garden of bodies. They block your exit, corner you in the bedroom. One tries to grab you and you pull your punch when you deck him in the jaw. One of the men pulls out a knife, which does surprise you—whatever happened to monologuing or at least a question or two asking who you are? These men go straight to killing: one man stabs you and breaks the blade against your ribs. You smile. Now they see you. You just think for help and a door of light appears in the room \ your teammates step through, and even though half of them are barefoot, smell like gin and cigarettes and someone else's sex from the night before, they heard you call and came running. You couldn't ask for more.

The Willpower Man says danger

is every day. I run to it
like fire across crosses,
like townsfolk to trees
to attend American justice. Soft
bodies lay on the floor
still asleep. Naked,
I step over them,
take a long drink
from the blue cup.
I don't know what's inside
but it's warm enough
and wakes me up.
The clothes I grab
fit just right. A blessing.
A white door appears.
And already I know
my marching orders. *Danger*
a voice says. Every time
I still step through /

The Telepath

touches the man's mind and reorders his blood and fury into lines she can read. He, along with the other men, did terrible things, and she's not sorry he's barely hovering above consciousness, only sorry that the victims are already gone and the men who stole them away are still alive, so now she must sift through his memories which are like swimming in shit: difficult to wash off. She tells herself this is good, useful work.

She could rummage through every malicious mind, help every victim's family. *What do they want with them?* Raise loved ones out of comas, find every killer and rapist. *Watch the road.* But why stop there? Why not simply rewire their minds—*watch the goddamn road*—so no one would ever dream of hurting another living creature again? Even if she could, they'd legislate her rights away if she was ever caught. Or worse. *It's not like they're human.*

on visibility

On the first train back into the city, you're doing everything you can to keep your back straight, your head up, while your teammate leans on your shoulder with heavy lids. You're both covered in blood and dirt. No one on the train looks at you, though they all know who you are. You gently jab your teammate to wake her up. *C'mon*, is all she says, waving you away before falling back to sleep, her mouth hanging open wide enough to let the spirit slip out of her. You offer stray smiles to anyone who will take them. A young mother and her child smile back. A young girl approaches you with a notepad and pen and it takes you a moment to realize she wants your name. You scribble something as the train signals the next stop and your teammate snaps awake on cue and quickly stands to get off. *You look like shit*, you tell her, and she laughs. *Can't all be invincible*, she replies before waving so long. You wave back as the doors close and you catch your own reflection waving you goodbye.

The Invincible Woman makes the front page

Here, like this, the photographer models how to properly hold the girl. Her blonde hair enters your mouth, you spit it out. The building behind you continues to burn. The photographer takes a series of shots. Your teammates are nearby coordinating with firefighters. *My job's easier than yours*, The Willpower Man jokes after the last flash, after they take the girl out of your hands and you instinctively tighten your grip before finally releasing her. No wonder, you'll think later: your profession and orphans go hand in hand.

The Precog

My sister loved math: how *x* could be any,
yet only, one thing. How you could prove
any variable with a little work. So when

grandma told my sister she couldn't go
to school but wouldn't say why, my sister
fumed in her room, worked ahead in her

used algebra book until the evening news
reported another school shooting. After that
we always listened to grandma but asked

why didn't she warn everyone else?
Grandma said she couldn't and cried
herself to sleep every night. It didn't stop

people from coming around every week
asking for lotto numbers and the best
time to leave their spouses, guarantees

for who would come home and who
wouldn't. Whenever neighbors came knocking
grandma would send us out with a twenty

to catch a movie at the second-run theater
or grab cokes and sandwiches at the corner
store, until an older girl jumped us and took

our money and our cokes and bloodied
my sister's nose, and when my sister asked
why? The girl shrugged *because.*

Sister and grandma argued that night
over why she didn't warn us. *If I told you
every time someone might whoop your ass*

you'd never leave the house. My sister
didn't hear her, but that night I dreamed
I paid someone two dollars to fly

then fell to my death. I asked
grandma if it was a sign. *No, baby,*
she said and sent me off to school.

The Invincible Woman goes to a party

One line can't erase it. Neither can smoke or edibles or the twenty-year scotch someone carelessly pours in your cup. A waste. The Willpower Man, his arm slung around your shoulder (more for helping him stand upright than for consolation), slurs that *soon we'll be the new normal*. You touch his face and smile before pushing him away. A werewolf whistles on the balcony and someone tells him to take it down a few notches. A young couple calls you into a room and asks if you'd like to spend the night with them. You'd like to indulge and forget what you witnessed that morning, what you commit every night. You check your pockets—you've got a few pills you've been saving and you're so close to feeling fucked up that you'd like to press on. But you know you'll never get there: oblivion's never been in your cards.

on restorative justice and Tony Danza

The Telepath sits cross-legged on the floor. You stand nearby. A cat rubs against the man's leg who just moments ago had pinned you against a tree, ready to smash your face. He looks around, not knowing how you escaped his grasp, and what happened to the tree, and whose home is this? It's a question he poses to the itchy carpet and the wood-paneled walls. As if in response, a younger version of the man runs inside, having just skipped school. He's no more than twelve in this memory and pays no attention to you, The Telepath, or the man still confused at his younger self brushing by him to sit on the sofa and turn on the tv. *What is this?* The man asks, angry now. You and The Telepath exchange a look: how does she want to play this? *It's okay*, The Telepath says, *everything's okay*. He steps towards her, and you step between them, but she just rolls her eyes—there's no danger here. *He's fine*, she says, which makes you feel a little embarrassed. The man takes in his surroundings again and stares at his younger self. *Do you have anything you'd like to say or share?* The Telepath asks him, but the man is already sitting on the sofa beside himself watching Angela berate Tony for not fixing the sink properly, and water is spraying everywhere, and wasn't it funny that Tony Danza's character was also named Tony, but the man always forgot it was Judith Light who played Angela until he would look her name up and then forget again. He laughs softly. *This was my favorite episode*, the man says, and you're not even sure this was an actual episode, but does it matter? When you leave here, you wonder if he's aware what will happen—what has already happened. You relax a little. His younger self sets the remote on the couch cushions between them. The four of you watch a few more minutes, before The Telepath asks, *Do you want to finish this episode?* He shakes his head, trying to hide a soft smile, *Nah*. Then he picks up the remote and turns off the tv.

rule of gravity

You're falling out a window fifty-eight floors up
hoping no one's below you. Even
in prayer, your own body comes last.

rehearsal

The guards are calm as they escort you down the hall into the small room. Five armed men stand nearby, their clammy hands tightly gripping .30-caliber rifles. A woman waits for you by the chair. You sit. The woman straps your arms and legs down with mechanical efficiency. Despite the cool room, she is sweating and will continue to sweat until this is routine. You (were) volunteered for this, which is something you now regret until you see your own face in these men and women who, like you, do work that dehumanizes you and the people you serve. You try to catch the woman's eyes, but she never looks at you directly. You almost say something and wonder if the next person who sits here would say anything. The supervising guard stares at you and the woman—and when you look his way, he does not break but gives a small nod: the only acknowledgement you've received. You don't nod back. She slips a hood over your head and pins a small red cloth over your heart. You hear the men ready their rifles. Aim.

The Telepath follows the bad man

Some nights she stands outside his home while he sleeps. It's not easy to change who a person is. Harder still to do nothing and see the tangerine walls and dead locusts piling on the table.

A distant memory: her hiding behind the slide, shots ringing in her ears. She willed her eyes to stay shut. It was then, for the first time, another person's mind opened to her: *Freedom. Victory. Death to the Great Satin.* Everything white hot. She just wanted it to stop. She wanted it to stop so bad, she imagined the bad man slowly turning the gun on himself, she just wanted it to stop, so she thought it. And in the thinking—POW!—change.

See her now: The Telepath standing outside the man's home, eyes closed, thinking what she might do.

The Invincible Woman enjoys her night off

You're full on kreteks and whiskey sours when the power goes out. The blue lights turn black, and the record shuts off right as Diana reassures *I don't need no cure*. Almost everyone on the dance floor stops, with a few people still swaying in silence. Just when you think about leaving, a woman sings *sweet, sweet, sweet, sweet love* into darkness and a few folks join in and start clapping a beat until everyone's grooving on the floor, spilling drinks they can't see. You go to check on your man in the backroom who's showing off playing pool—sinking each shot without touching the cue ball. One of his favorite tricks. The power cuts back on when you ask if he wants to split something to eat, and he flashes you a smile in the way men do when they'll devour anything you feed them. Tomorrow you'll both be hungover on the job, saving the world from itself for the thousandth time. But tonight, you're young and invincible. The lights turn red and low. You order a fried fish plate and the grease is so good, you lick your fingers clean.

The Telepath tries you on

Physicality has never been a problem, but once someone starts talking about astral planes and psychic energy, you're already checked out. So when the villain shut down your mind and your friend picked you up, poured herself inside you, wound you up, and marched you across the field, you told yourself you could not care less. It wasn't just you, after all; she was inside all your teammates, and if she lost, it's quite possible you and the country and the world would've ended.

But then you remembered the Cadre of Sinister Intent who took control of your bodies for days. One switched places with you, banished you in his body while he strode in yours, did what he wanted with your body, got to be invincible for a while, *unstoppable* he said when you were finally able to switch back and gain control of yourself, after you had collared him and put him in cuffs. Your leader offered a series of therapy sessions for everyone to discuss how it felt to be back in your own body as if you had just arrived back at your own home after being absent for a month and smelling the old ducts and kitchen smells you had lived with for so long you forgot they were there, and now you couldn't stop smelling old food someone forgot to throw out.

So when your friend apologized for taking you over, you knew she had good reason and wanted to empathize, but instead you blurted out, *Never again*.

tales to astonish

~

\ You know something's off as soon as you step through the door and everyone is just a little taller, no one looks remotely like you, and there's only one moon in the sky. You were sent to stop a group from blowing up an oil pipeline, but there's no group, no pipeline, and everyone's looking at you and your teammates as if you're strangers in your own country. Then your teammate that creates doors sheepishly admits that sometimes his doors don't always work quite right: when he means to travel through just space, he also crosses into other planes of reality. *Great*, your well-meaning leader says, meaning that you're in trouble he can't outthink. To nip it in the bud, you all decide to simply leave through another door /\ but you come out in the same city under the same single-moon sky and the same people look at you as if you're a threat. Your leader decides to find your headquarters in this country that is yours but not yours, which is a terrible idea since you're not from around here, which surely means your home is not your home but someone else's. But—your leader reasons—you're good guys, so chances are the other yous in this world are probably also good guys and would be willing to help as much as you would be willing to help some other version of you that arrived by accident in your world. *That depends*, you argue, *how much would I like this other me?*

~

Not much, it turns out. That's not fair. When you and your teammates arrive and meet your other selves, you're not surprised that you're a tall, attractive, hazel-eyed man who leads this version of your team and is all too willing to help you and whose face adorns a newly minted two-dollar coin, but you don't know what this says about your world or this one. *You know exactly what it says*, The Willpower Man says after you/they manage to help you/us find your way back home after helping them stop an alien invasion. For a few weeks, you'll swear off relying on your teammate's doors every time you want to avoid taking the train or grabbing a drink from your favorite bar with just a few steps, but then you find yourself and The Telepath sharing a cigarette on a bare-bones patio surrounded by people too drunk and thirsty to take you home, so she sends out a little whisper to your teammate to pick you both up / and drop you off \ at The Willpower's Man apartment and you go back to taking everything for granted.

meanwhile...

Don't you feel lonely all the time? I say to myself. Even with the windows rolled down, I'm sweating in a car I've never owned in my world. The name *Edsel* stitched in the steering wheel. *Whose car is this?* I ask, trying to change the subject, already knowing the answer. *Mine*, I say, staring at me. Soon, the clear sky will fill with invaders and we know what comes next. *Do they always send you off on your own too?* I ask myself. *Yeah*, I reply, staring ahead. I'm beautiful. I'm sitting in the driver's seat, answering questions we both know the answers to. *Maybe I could visit your world someday?* It probably won't happen, but what can I say? I'm lonely all the time, and I'm almost sure I'll die alone—this profession all but guarantees it. I watch myself tap the steering wheel, look out the driver's side window, and note the blue sky, not a hostile in sight. *Come here*, I say.

a   A   a

The television on the kitchen counter reports a homicide—rolls footage of a boy too young to understand his gift who accidently tosses his friend too high into the sky before he falls in the neighbor's backyard and breaks his neck. The Telepath sips hibiscus mint and considers the moral implications of removing rot only you can smell. The men on tv argue if the boy qualifies as human. Fresh off work, I strip off my suit and throw on a pair of jeans and a t-shirt so old I don't recognize the faded *Made in America* tag, though what remains seems intentional, like a poorly thought-out logo. I haven't slept all night. I greet her in the kitchen, pour already cold coffee in a cup, and lean on the counter, trying to focus on the men on tv who agree the boy they refuse to see as a boy should be charged as a man. She tries not to pry, but she can't help but peek inside my head—I open the door wide. She steps in—hesitant at first, then smells my wet violence. *We shouldn't*, she thinks. *It's alright*, I think back.

The Telepath tells your fortune

Your man chucks men across a field like frisbees without touching them. Your man has night sweats. Your man smiles at people who try to kill him. After a long night of drinks, your friend tells you, *Every night he dreams he's human and living in a condo with a young daughter and a canary, and he hates that it's a dream he can't stop having.* Drunk, you're bemused and a little jealous. You haven't recalled a single dream in years. *How about me?* you ask. *What do I dream?* Your friend says you dream yourself awake. You mishear her: you dream yourself a wake.

I dream about my wake! You yell. Your friend could correct you but doesn't. You shout it over and over as if you just realized this truth about yourself. *I dream about my wake!* You shout at the men smoking outside. They say nothing but hold their drinks tighter. *I dream about my wake!* You shout at the drunk couple arguing in front of the house. You startle them into silence, and they hurry back inside. It makes sense, of course, dreaming about things you cannot have. Before you were old enough to go to school you once had a dream you were flying, but you couldn't control it, so you were zooming all over the sky, almost crashing into the trees, your own house, your mother below. It was terrifying. You woke up sweating and relieved it was only a dream and prayed to god you could have that dream again.

men on fire

Everything leans towards cruelty: you
and your friend walking from the local
bakery full on beignets and coffee

when a burning man falls from the sky
and craters the street corner. You're alive
but rattled. Others are already bones

licked clean from fire. The man
is confused. It hurts to look at him covered
in flame. You don't want to kill him (but

you could; you always could) so you hold
out your hand, slowly walk towards him.
He raises one arm and you can't tell

if he's pointing or offering his hand.
Your clothes catch fire—you imagine
both of you walking away from this

alive. The burning man cocks his head
to one side as if he's never stood
in the middle of his own destruction.

Then a blast of light explodes from
his right temple. He collapses, dead.
Amazing men hover over your head

before touching down and apologizing:
who knew he'd land so far away
we're sorry we couldn't get here sooner
everything's fine.

The Telepath turned broken record

She saw the terrible things the president had done, so she did what any good person would do: wrote letters to her local representatives, started a petition, made signs, wrote poems. We told her it was a shame. A shame the president could have allowed such things. But it's not like he did it with his own hands, and he had done good things too, and who could say anymore what was true? *I've got the memory right here!* she said and projected it across the gray skies of our minds. But wasn't there a world to save somewhere? An invasion to repel? *But*, she said. Then an evil professor took over a small town, so she and her teammates were called in to save the day. When they killed the professor, we threw them a parade. *But no more bad talk about the president, or else…* we said. As if great men couldn't make mistakes. As if she wasn't also unclean.

our leader

is a good man, but a bit of a careerist. Every move we make is orchestrated to improve our standing, earn a little more acclaim, good press. So when we decide to finally revisit our old school, he declines, *I'd rather not*. We get it, it's history for him, and he'd rather leave it behind, but it's history for us too, which means, like this school,

it hasn't changed much, except now all the lockers are empty, and the classrooms still have the ghosts of strategies on chalkboards, main arteries mapped on plastinated bodies. We were told we were the inaugural class, that we would be the change our country needed. It is easy enough

to enter the headmaster's office, completely sealed off, except through a small window. Easy to possess a songbird to view inside and make a door / and walk \ right in. He is not surprised to see us, though refuses to give us the names of students who came after us, who may still be here, though it doesn't matter; we enter his mind and take what we need. *Don't you know how proud we are of you?* is what men say when they think they're ready for you and find themselves lacking. We almost turn him over to the proper authorities, until we remembered he was once considered a proper authority.

respite

~

The Willpower Man sits on the stoop, drinking bottled water. Two children fly overhead, suspended by his sheer will, while a line of thirty children stretch in front of him, jostling each other for a turn.

~

One boy pushes the girl in front of him, accuses her of cutting. You pick him off the ground with one hand. *If you want, I can make you fly too*, you say. The boy grows silent, dangling in the air like a kitten. Then you see the girl he punched slip another girl in front of her two dollars. She sees you watching her and smiles. *My momma's gonna whoop me if you stretch my collar*, the boy says. You set him down, wishing you could be anywhere else than here bouncing fourth and fifth graders standing in line for a chance to fly.

~

Aw, leave those kids alone, The Willpower Man says as two children gently touch down on the sidewalk in front of him. *We've been here for almost an hour*, you say, wondering how long it takes for your leader to have his future read by someone's grandmama on the fifth floor. A tradition he's been doing for almost as long as you've known him: fresh after emancipation, he found her (such a strange verb that contains an entire story you'll never know) and based not only his entire life on their annual visits, but—you suspect—your lives as well.

~

Eight more children get to fly before your leader comes down and tells you to come with him. You and your man exchange a look—this has never happened before. Even your leader doesn't know what to say as you climb the four flights of stairs to knock on the door and greet the woman who looks younger than you imagined aside from her gray locs spilling out of a bright green and gold scarf. Her body is soft and small. The smell of bacon grease stored in a jar by the oven hits you as you step inside. *Take a seat*, she says, gesturing to two chairs around the small kitchen table, before she looks at you again. Her face cracks and her hand shakes as she touches your shoulder. You both wait in that moment.

~

Go back outside, she says as if you were a child in trouble. You look at your leader who only shrugs and says with his eyes, *Do what she says*.

~

You swear the line has doubled since you were upstairs, but you resume your role, playing bouncer and pitching stones into the sun anytime a kid bets they could throw further than you. Three gunshots ring through the block. You shield the nearest children with your body, and try to determine where the shots came from, but there's too much echo between buildings, it's impossible to tell. The Willpower Man snaps to attention and stands up as if he's ready to rocket towards the source. You put a hand on his shoulder to ground him—wherever it is, you know the tragedy has already happened—it's happening right now, then you look up and see the girls' legs flailing, their arms reaching for hands that are not there, falling from the sky, paying the price for The Willpower Man's distraction. You reach out, shoving him out of the way to make your arms as wide as you can and catch both girls. Their eyes are shut tight and don't open until you gently lay them on the sidewalk, and before the other kids swarm the girls to ask them if they're alright, what it felt like to almost die, to fall from the sky, one girl opens her eyes and you recognize each other. *The bribe was worth it*, she says with her smile. You smile back.

██████ History Month

The young boy on stage sings *Amazing Grace*, and each note turns into your oldest olfactory memory. Everyone is crying and applauding. The judges' table asks him the first question. Standing near the back of the crowd, your man calls him a glorified scratch-and-sniff. *He'll never make the cut.* You punch him hard in the shoulder. Any time one of you is on stage it should be an occasion for joy. But he's not wrong, you both know it's all for show: none of these contestants will advance. They've already decided who will win. They told you that morning. Still, the night sky is breezy and cool, full of stars you can just make out this far from the stage. Your friend shows up with overpriced beers and asks what she missed. *Nothing*, your man says, but she can't hear him over the boos and groans: a young man turns water into Hennessy and takes a drink. You hold out your cigarette for your friend to take and close your eyes. Close the stars. The judges adjust the blank papers on their desk. *She looks promising*, your friend says. You drink and watch the girl onstage bend down and lightly touch the cat's head—transforming him into a dying fish—then a lumbering bear—then a hawk that takes flight and is off before anyone can applaud, before anyone realizes it's not coming back.

on the clock

You're watching the performance onstage when people begin shouting in either pain or fear. There are no shots fired, but your friend puts her hand on your shoulder. You can't see the violence, but you can see its effects: people running from the front of the stage which has now collapsed, and you don't see the contestants or judges anywhere, including your leader, so it's down to you. *Call it*, The Willpower Man says.

no more water

You and the boy are hurtling through clouds. He'll be dead by the time you hit earth—the only question is how: by his hand or yours. The crowd looks up and points and mistakes this dying for performance. You feel the heat inside his chest. He would have preferred to die on his feet, take as many people with him as he can. *You don't have to do this*, you say, knowing he does. *Look at them*, the boy says. *Look at what they've done to us.* Throngs of people below are recording you, taking pictures. No one is going anywhere. Your grip tightens. It happens fast. The boy flashes you a joyless grin before he breaks apart, burning everything away. People below gawk at what they think is a firework display gone wrong. You drop like a stone and hit the ground naked and unharmed with nothing in your arms.

.

stranger things

I've seen white folks do the strangest
things: park and block thru traffic,
leave the engine running, get outraged
at their own blindness to bad people
who do bad things, place their dogs
on the baker's counter, die of old age.

on language

Let's call the boy a terrorist in his final act, even though it was a failed bombing since he didn't so much as explode but burst into fire and light harmlessly above us. But we know his intentions: so let's call it a terrorist attack, let's exercise caution, get bipartisan support, take necessary steps, detain every boy who can turn into stars.

a different world

Go then, there are other worlds
than these, the boy says
before falling into another book /
somewhere more comforting
for our brutal imagination
where everything we think is true,
is. We try not to dwell on the times
when we are a different us—
and let's not say *better*, because
that means we don't have it good
here (cue the prophet who said
every lived life is worth living)
even if the life over there resides
in a country you can't name or
failed to transform
into the inevitable cruelty we live in
now and now I understand the man
on the bridge, the woman with a gun,
how much easier it is to destroy yourself
than change the world. It should give
you comfort that there's a changed
you out there that's not at all you
and doesn't care to look back.

old lions

i

Lobo and Waku down another shot
of rye at the lobby bar, knowing
they'll be passed over for every award
save maybe a lifetime achievement,
unless Luke Cage or Catwoman-
as-Eartha-Kitt win again. T'Challa,

half-drunk, buys rounds for nearby
tables, loud as he wants to be, while
the Dogs of War stand guard, each
with a powder blue pocket square
covering their hearts. Everyone

two drinks from ejection.
Mari McCabe sings *Nice Work
if You Can Get It* but pours
too much blue and not enough
black. *It's bad comedy,*
Lobo quips. *A cowboy
and a prince walk into a bar.*

ii

An empty bottle of Bulleit
reminds Waku of his tribe,
long gone: their gray faces
surrendering themselves
for their hero / dying for their
negro / a reprint prince
without a kingdom. Might keep
him in circulation though.
Might get a reboot, might get
a Halloween costume.

iii

Most Sensational, Most Startling,
Blackest Superhero, The Hardest
Motherfucker Alive, The Realest
Nigga On the Block: T'Challa wins
them all. Nothing to take home,
Waku still applauds the night's end.

iv

Lobo only wants to know who the judges are.

the golden age

They had just returned from defeating a rogue star in a contest of riddles and feats of strength. We threw them a parade. We missed them. We loved them and we were afraid. Covered in confetti, someone asked, *Can you find my cat?* Someone asked, *Can you find my daughter?* Someone asked, *Can you recover my newspaper?* But they said they were tired and asked if they could rest for a day. We hated them then and felt ashamed for hating, for imagining the rogue star hurtling back to its own galaxy, threatening to supernova some other pitiful planet without her heroes. Someone started a fire. Someone murdered the parishioners. Then we remembered the circus was in town, recalled the trapeze artist the night before had almost died, but was caught by her ankle at the last minute by her own daughter. *Wasn't that something?* We pinched ourselves. *Wasn't that amazing?*

II

promotion

You take a line of cocaine because why not? Your life is infinite and endless and not your own and sometimes you wish you could just close your eyes and never open them and the god you once fought told you that you'll outlive the earth and nearly everyone on it and you'll one day meet that god again. You take another line. You want to chew carbon to coal but you lack sufficient heat. The woman next to you uses a business card an aspiring hero just gave her whose name she's already forgotten except for when she rubs a smudge of powder off the name Lucretia. *Lucretia should change her name if she wants to make it in this business.* A young man takes off his shirt and tells you he's your biggest fan. He holds a beer can in his hand and it melts into a puddle of hot metal on the floor. *So do I make the cut?* He asks, and you realize this is a demonstration. For what, you don't know. When you don't say anything right away, he says *fuck you then* and storms off, still shirtless. You want to grab him by his arm and hurl him into the next state. *Congratulations*, the woman sitting next to you says, suddenly recognizing who you are, and offers you another line.

tryouts

> For those of us who live at the shoreline / standing upon
> the constant edges of decision / crucial and alone
>
> —Audre Lorde from "A Litany for Survival"

> With that jive bunch of turkeys in the JLA? Forget it!!
>
> —Black Lightning from *Justice League of America*, no. 173

There's one boy on fire and another drowning. You only get to save one
for your final exam, so you lift the wet boy from the lake and don't realize
your mistake until Superman touches down. *Sorry son, we can't have*

someone who chooses their own over everyone else. The boy's brown fingers
hold tight to your emblem, leave wet impressions on your chest. Next
year the same, and the same after that. Every time you choose wrong. Blame it

on empire. Superman, his arm wrung around your neck, *We're trying*
to save the world here, his eyes pure blue, confirming what you
already knew: you always save the ones never meant to survive.

Welcome to The Amazing, Invincible Woman!
Hope you survive the experience!

When you ascend the stage to take your place among your new team, you don't know what to say. You didn't prepare a speech, or a list of people to thank, or anything, really. You would think this is old hat for you, but the throngs of reporters and journalists tell you otherwise. Never mind you were known before this fanfare, along with your old teammates who it seems everyone has already forgotten. People are taking photos and yelling questions and there's a podium positioned in front of your new leader, who is unlike your old leader in that he wears a full skintight costume with bright colors that show off his well-built body that you wouldn't mind having for a night. *Here she is, folks!* Your new leader says. A person in the front tells her friend, *She's so pretty, and that hair!* Your new leader raises your arm as if you've won a bout and says, *Welcome to The Amazing, Invincible Woman!* The crowd erupts in camera flashes and questions:

How strong are you? Did you even apply for the job? I didn't see you compete! Is it true that nothing can kill you? Can we trust you? Where are you from? Who are you? What's your name? What's your real name?

The Telepath discovers a new gift

Every week, she walked to the corner café that served Nutella and banana crepes so sweet she drank her coffee black. Sometimes people who ordered after her got their food first. Young girls would sometimes take the other chair from her table without asking. Adjuncting at the local community college was the most stable work she could find after quitting her last job, even though her students never remembered her name, only called her *Miss* or *Teacher* or *Miss Teacher*. She wondered if this was a side effect of her gift, turn it into something she could control: making herself invisible. It could be useful: to bump into people at the bank and only receive a blank stare instead of recognition that she was someone they once _____. Maybe she could extend this gift to others, let her people retire peacefully. Then a sudden laugh erupted from her and a few folks turned to look. She couldn't help it. Who had she ever known to retire?

on acceptance

The bipartisan crowd applauds when the Governor pins a medal on you. He's not delicate with the sharp point because he assumes you can't feel it pierce your chest. He's wrong on both counts: the pin can't pierce you at all, just folds under its own failure to hurt you. But you can feel the warm metal, it just doesn't bother you. You've been practicing since you were a child: learning how to turn it off and on like blinking. Now you don't feel anything at all. Now you do. It's a gift. You're here because you helped a boy kill only himself. You wanted to refuse the medal, the pageantry, but were told to think of your position—what it would look like if you refused to appear, what it means to people watching that you're the first of your kind to receive such an honor. *The Invincible Woman Breaking Barriers*, a headline reads. You're on the capitol steps, white columns flanking you, making you feel small, making you wish you could take off into the sky. But despite your many gifts, you cannot fly.

on power

This is not who we are.

—Everyone

All my friends take their pick: promotion or fame, ignored or hung. You don't hear me dream but believe all the myths: I've got hearts of stone of steer of buck of horse of ape of course I bleed in watermelon and grape. Y'all can't touch New World numbers but use me and mine to keep the lights on. We was busy fighting villains | getting tenure | giving talks | praying every Sunday for relief that the First and Fifteenth can't provide. I'm freelance now—yank the legs from under the would-be robbers and run the white-collar white collars out of every town. But I can be kindness, be fire, the smoke, the field, the heat. Can bend rivers with my hand, bring oceans to land, let it swallow you all until it's had its fill. You think that would make us even? Level the field? I was raised to not raise a hand against you, to protect you from *foreign actors who don't have our best interests at heart*. I'd like to know who does, and who is included in *our*.

The Amazing

We got kids to feed. Mortgages to pay.
Deals to make. Fuck a seat

at the table, we buying the table.
We hitting Beyoncé numbers. Our marshmallow

faces soften in your milk. We pair slick
adjectives with slick nouns and catch

falling planes. We don't order bottle service,
we buy the distillery, get a cut every time

you make an Incredible Hulk. We working
on copyrighting the drink, the name, the character,

the media. Muthafuckas just *think* green,
we getting paid. You feel us? You'd like to.

The Telepath consoles The Willpower Man

I've done a bad thing, he says to The Telepath. She asks him what. *Take a look*, he says. She finds a clean carpet, an open window, an empty glass, and a surprising lack of gore. She's never been great at consolation so she only nods in agreement, reassures him that he did what he felt was right and that was enough.

Could you take it away? he asks. She takes offense at this—him finding her after all this time, just to cure his remorse. Had she always been viewed this way? When they were children, she had to suppress memories after certain jobs. *Something to help everyone sleep*, her handler told her. She obliged because she wanted to be a good team player, and she feared what would happen if they felt she was no longer useful. And even after they rebelled and struck out on their own, she considered the consequence of removing the dust covers off all of those old missions and letting everything flood back into knowing. Their leader agreed this would be a bad idea, so she never wiped away her wiping, and carried the guilt under her tongue like a stone.

Her hand on The Willpower Man's hand, she decides to gently massage the memory. She will later regret this. But for now, she only wants to help ease the haunted look in her friend's eyes, the assuredness that this memory—left unchecked—will spread to others, and soon everywhere he looks, he'll feel, not shame, but anger at his actions: the dead man in the memory had done unspeakable things, and wasn't the world better off without him? And if without, then who else might be better cast off now?

The Telepath gently strips the carpet, folds the frayed curtains, closes the windows, locks all the doors, sands the floor away until it's bare, until nothing is left but the bones of the house, of the people, everything alabaster white. *There, there.*

The Invincible Woman has a case of the Mondays

The new job is more difficult than you expect. It's not the work, not exactly. Just the other day, you were launched at a nuclear missile and detonated it in the air, sparing the small Eastern European nation from being wiped off the map. You were quarantined for weeks before they could make sure you wouldn't spread contamination. You told them you weren't a danger, but they didn't take you at your word. You're placed right beside your new leader on stage at every press conference, signaling your country's commitment to preserving democracy and a warning to all foreign bad actors. Behind the scenes, you're forced to pore over dossiers, memorize names of reporters and politicians and foreign diplomats so you *sound like you know what you're talking about.* You argue that's not the job, your new boss argues it is. Eventually, you confuse one diplomat's name for another, and evening pundits openly ask, *Should we trust people who don't know the difference between Sweden and France?* A panelist reminds them that you're not technically *people*, meaning human, so maybe you deserve a pass. They laugh.

birthday cake

I never had a nemesis that inspired fear, or some opposite-man that could counter my will. Even if I had a weakness, I wouldn't share it. But I'll admit I never understood the monkey's paw, the genie's lamp, magic stones, or cosmic cubes—there's always a cost to transformation and I want nothing to do with any of it. I once argued against our old leader when he instructed me to return the artifact back to its place and have The Telepath erase my memory, so no one would ever know where to find it again (*but wouldn't she?* I wanted to ask but knew better than to question all the things she knew/didn't know). Oh, I secretly wished for all kinds of shit: to see my enemies crushed, your undying love, a perfect world, but someone somewhere would pay for it. And isn't that what's gotten us here—people paying the price for someone else's wishful thinking?

on sorrow & joy

What number am I thinking? Her mother used to ask her every morning before driving her to the new school where all the students stared at her and wondered why she didn't look like them. They called her a banana; she didn't know why. In their heads, she saw crudely drawn fruit with straight lines for eyes. She ate her lunches in homeroom with her teacher who didn't mind but asked her questions like, *How long have you been here? It's a shame what happened at that other school. That would never happen here.* Her teacher was well meaning but didn't truly believe it, and it broke The Telepath's heart to know this. Though her teacher did believe she could protect The Telepath if it came down to it and routinely shared her meal when The Telepath would finish her lunch and was still hungry. *This girl can eat*, her teacher used to think without any malice. And though she was old enough to know she shouldn't invade her teacher's privacy, it would take a few years before she understood how rare it was to be in the presence of someone free of judgement, resentment, and all too eager to share a ripe orange or double-chocolate cookie.

next

We pass around photos of applicants:
ground-pounder, flyer, speed, light

telekinesis. It bothers you how quickly
we categorize and reject. You call it

a waste to see such talent thrown
in the trash, but this is how it's done.

You're a fool if you think we're the only power
in this world. There are other, rarer variants. Normal

everyday people don't care how many times
we save them, a recent poll says they trust

the police more than us. That should worry you:
what they'll do out of fear.

in blackest day, in brightest night

three boys turn blackbird, break church windows like shots fired, interrupting my midnight walk—half drunk and singing Al Green under the artificial light of a moon. I enter the church and find the dead man by the front-row pews. He's still holding a gasoline can with a dumb look of shock on his face and three bird-sized holes through his chest. I close my eyes and can feel every shard of glass littered in the dirt and piece the windows back together, able to make Mary whole again as easily as I can take the man apart. It's sobering work: leaving no trace, making the dead disappear. I'm fearless, not brave: an American contradiction. I love my countrymen most when their eyes roll black.

The Telepath quits her day job

She didn't know his name or the shape of his face but saw the color of his better world: bulletproof, untested, and true. That thought invited more: the morning commuters, her students, the men in the bookstore, everyone thinking, *What happened to my country*. Her brain became a comments page. Her nose bled every day. She considered putting a bullet in her head. Instead she bought a notebook and copied every stray thought. Soon she had a closet full, then a bedroom, then a house, then an editor called and called the book *People of the World*. You bought a copy but didn't realize you were your own favorite poem. You read it to all your friends.

assembly

Sneaking a cigarette around the corner from the east gym doors, he wasn't eager to see the special guests, though it did get him out of fourth period, so he decided not to skip and see them in person. He had never seen one up close before, only on television. His teachers always remarked how they were a sign of progress, how they represented *us*. He called bullshit. They never came to his neighborhood, never stopped any robberies or muggings near the Rite Aid or Walmart parking lot just a few blocks away or brought home his uncle who was pulled over and never seen again. Even this school function was simple charity—they weren't coming to tell the student body that they *too can be up here if you work hard enough*, but to show him and his friends that some things are inherited under the guise of being earned. *A rising tide lifts all boats*, his algebra teacher said, as if all boats could retain the same amount of water. No, if he was going to fly, he'd have to find his own way, 'cause he'd be damned if he was going to stay here.

The Telepath listens to the flowers and trees

It's difficult to admit that the world would be better off without you. Worse to be told. Yet she heard it clear as day: watering her chrysanthemums, hearing them gossip about her neighbors, how careless they were on garbage day, how often the waste of their lives spilled outside their containers, how the world seemed to be nothing but containers—for humans, for their waste, their small lives, their constant deaths. She knew all this of course, just as she knew when the mums called her *one of the good ones* that they didn't really need her when they had rain. It hurt her feelings at first, but she agreed to listen more to the trees, flowers, squirrels and goslings, every spider mending its broken web, every walked dog, every small thing slowly walking towards its own hurried end.

new gods

I'm just drinking a cup of coffee when the horse-drawn carriage trots the tourists by and someone decides I'll save the world or ruin it. Everybody a novelist before they step out the door, but I can't hate, y'all putting up real numbers—uploading a hundred manifestos before strapping up and walking into their nearest Dollar Store. Y'all love myth: turn us into something we ain't every day: if I can be more, then I can be less. Let me jump the gun, transform myself first. I can be as merciless as you. Pay my mother's mortgage or kick rocks. Someone holds my hand, shoots off that old chestnut about pens being mightier: *Violence never solves anything*. History disagrees. Like any evening or book, killing does conclude—which isn't the same as *solves* but provides resolution, if not revolution, which we're told never lasts. You need us to define who you are. You believe we need you the same. We don't. It's a lesson you won't unlearn.

The Telepath attends a book club

There are bear claws and single serving bottles of orange juice concentrate. The group—a mix of retirees, single parents, faculty, and a few students from the community college she once taught at—talk in earnest about the author's message of equality and how even though it was written forty years ago, it still rings true today. They cut small glances towards The Telepath when they discuss how _____ *don't live in the same America due to the institutionally and legislatively backed discriminatory policies that still run rampant today.* A young man goes back for a second bear claw. A woman excuses herself when they discuss the graphic scene of a man brutally murdered by police after being stopped for expired plates and accidentally shocking one of the officers. Someone recognizes The Telepath and suggests reading her book of poems. She politely requests they choose another book, which offends the book club. *She thinks she's better than us*, someone thinks. *She shouldn't even be here, what if someone attacks the library? I've never seen her around before. Can you hear me? Are you listening to my thoughts right now? Please leave us alone.* The Telepath excuses herself. Someone suggests another book they could read—it just came out and it's already a finalist for a few awards. Everyone agrees it's a fine idea.

exhibition

The famous artist takes you through room after room of photographs of power poses, women in flight, men in tights adorned with dust and blood. You drink sauvignon blanc out of a plastic cup and study yourself stretched on canvas, rendered in charcoal, covering one wall. People stand and admire this—the largest piece in the gallery. The artist's husband nudges you, scotch in hand from a bottle locked in his office and says you must be thrilled to see yourself on display. His wife was jealous that she never got a chance to photograph you, had to settle for her own imagination. He tells you how he bought the gallery for a song, and how rewarding it felt to finally open the doors and put the space to good use, and how the whole neighborhood is being revitalized, and jokes maybe one day they won't even need people like you. You nod politely and excuse yourself. No one sees you step outside, light a cigarette, and gaze across the street at the new bank where a tenement once stood. The windows are so clean you could step right through. You wonder whose job it is to clean glass so well it disappears. Without thinking, you hold your cigarette out for someone to take, but no one's there.

Astro Boy blues

rap your knuckles on my skin   show
me that you care   you
can't jostle my hair   you
can oil the black metal   make
it shine   clean
me up like your own ten-year-old boy   if
I don't love you   don't
take it personal   you're
the wrong shape   my
friends have Pythagorean angles   slice
open hands when they shake   they
say accept no substitutions   I'm
the improvement on the real McCoy   I'm
the AC on a high noon day   use
me in place of the natural breeze   I'll
keep you cool

Beast Boy

    My costar already on set, the director motions me

into the frame.
                  I'm slicked in baby oil
                  & unlaced Timbs
as she takes me in one hand,
herself in the other.
                  The backlight washes out her fingers

against my chest (crank your Black
              levels to HIGH).

    I rub her white-stockinged thigh

as the eye zooms back

        & my body becomes a bull
          not fully, but enough

    so she can bury her hands in my fur
    until I transform back to man
           & can you see?
           The monstrous seam

where hide gives way to skin. I've been
        many things: birds & snakes,

buffalo & buck
    for the camera's thrill. I'm a crossover

   kill. There's not much I haven't

seen, haven't fucked,
haven't made beautiful
     by placing myself beside it.

   After I've spent, I'm all white-
     tailed kite—a flurry cooing

       & clasped in my costar's small pale hands.

People call me a sellout, a monster, a beast, tomorrow

I'll be another animal, a different kind
      of miracle.

on vulnerability

You give a moment of thanks when you pull the knife out of your side, feeling light-headed at the sight of your own blood. The villain of the week is pummeling your new leader, sapping a bit of his strength, which is considerable. You're not sure how her gift works—maybe she absorbs someone's strength through proximity or touch or empathy, hence the blood on your hands, which is beginning to subside. Already your body remembers its natural state. If there's one thing you're good at, it's pressure.

You gamble if you hammer her hard enough you'll overwhelm her before she adds your power to her own. It pays off: you choke her out until she falls asleep. Super strength or invincibility or no, everyone must breathe.

The day saved, you think that's the end of it until the news breaks with video and photos of you aiding the police in subduing and beating your own kind. You're called a traitor. A sellout. People recall how you once blew up a small boy and posts clips and photos online. Your new leader says it's an old story, *something humans do to sow distrust in us, it'll blow over*. During a town hall, the incumbent calls you all *dangerous animals, a menace even to themselves*, and he promises *to clean up their kind*, and no one seems to take it seriously. *When I'm elected, we won't need them anymore.*

The Telepath finds the bright side

When she looked to the sky, this is what she saw: scores of children wired to artificial moons orbiting our world: batteries to last a lifetime. What she saw made her scream, made her shout from her home, but we didn't listen. She tried broadcasting the truth directly into our minds, but we called it fake news. We weren't about to give up our lunar-powered world full of free and wonderful light. Someone pointed at The Telepath and said, *Isn't it past time we did something about them?* And when someone said *them*, we knew what they meant. We sent her death threats, told her to keep her mouth shut. We streamed gasoline through the backyard garden, trampled the mums, huddled on the back porch and struggled with the match until the neighbors saw. When that failed, the direct approach—we bought torches and pitchforks (call us old-fashioned), strapped on our guns, and marched down the block under moonlight and knocked on the front door. *She moved out*, the neighbors said. *Good riddance*, we replied. We kissed our flags for good luck.

population boom

Every dead child comes back. The cities crowd out from north to south. Blink and they're fine, blink again and they look exactly how we left them under the water, under the earth, bound and destroyed. The ones burned look fine, except when you squint and they resemble walking ash in the form of a girl. Our heroes are somewhere finding the cause. Though some of the boys seem grateful they can breathe again (*Can they?* someone asks. *Can they breathe again? Or are we just imagining, because it's what we now want?*), other children fear that we'll put them right back in the ground, that the world hasn't changed. They eat our food but can't fill themselves, so they eat and they eat and they eat and they eat and whole cities are devoured and they don't mean to do it, but they're hungry, and we never fed them properly when they were alive, or even after we killed them the first time. Our heroes are finding the cause. Look, we love the dead. We love giving eulogies, writing elegies, adorning stones with flowers, and blinking back tears every time we're reminded that the same wrongs that put them in the ground keep us here. Dear lord, the dead are coming back and it's too much. The planet can't sustain this, the wheels will fall off. We arm ourselves and walk the streets and hunt for the dead. We feel bad at first, but it gets easier with every shot. Who needs heroes? If we're fast enough, they won't know what they've been missing. This is mercy. This is us choosing.

III

the new rules

_____ are not _____.

If your mother is a _____, you are also a _____.

If your father is a _____, you are also a _____.

If you can turn into a bird, you can turn into a gun.

Even if attacked, a _____ may not strike a person without legal and moral consequence.

Unless state or federally sanctioned, _____ may not assemble unless at least one person is present.

_____ are not permitted to marry.

If you can dance, you can do as you're told.

Anything a _____ sees or witnesses is inadmissible in court.

All _____ must register themselves with the National Registry.

All registered _____ are considered deadly weapons.

If you can breathe air, you can breathe dirt.

early retirement

~

You tell her you're going out of town for a little while, but you've been together long enough she knows what that really means. *I thought you quit*, is all she says.

~

You're almost finished sanding and re-staining her wooden deck when she brings you a cold beer along with one for herself. You clink and admire the spirea bushes she just planted in the front yard. She's sweating much harder than you, but you put the cold bottle to your head because just looking at her makes you feel warm. *It looks nice*, you tell her, though you fear they'll die just like the ones she planted last year. *I didn't prune them enough*. She says this as if she read your mind, and it gives you pause, but you know she has no gifts, not even a green thumb. You've made this joke before and she pouted for a day, so now you keep it to yourself, but how relieved you are at her clumsiness at all things, her inability to roast a chicken, her willingness to not throw it in your face that only one of you is considered human.

~

You should move in, she says. You tell her, as always, that's a terrible idea. And she agrees that it's indeed a terrible idea for her to move in with you, but no one has to know if you live with her. You explain, not for the first time, how people will know. They just will. It's how trouble works. And your life has always been trouble. It's a secondary gift your people share, you tell her, and she argues that trouble is common to the human experience. *You're not special.*

~

Her soft parts are your favorite, your hands on her stomach, the inside of her thigh caught in your mouth. She's younger than you by ten years, but it's not noticeable, because you stopped aging some years back, and even if it was, so what? You joke that your real gift is to be able to keep up with her, and she just says *huh* and looks at you as if you just ate the last slice of sweet potato pie.

~

I think you should go, she says. And you're not sure how to respond. She's right, you should go, and you will go, but it's strange to hear her finally say it. The television shows people breaking windows and tumbling inside. You could get there in about fifteen minutes. What scares you the most is that the violence is already so close. If you moved in, it would be closer. You'd invite it in your home.

The Willpower Man

Men fly every day. Don't believe
me? Watch me point my finger
like a gun, mouth *bang* & send
a man out the window. Falling
or flying, the only difference
is intent. The man walking
envies the man in the sky
until he hits the ground.
There's a better way, our betters
tell us, everyone desperate
for change without changing
a goddamn thing. The people in charge
level charges against me. My people
never touch dirt. We dream
of killing until we do
and plummet back to earth.
When I was young, I was beautiful
& legion. We filled the sky.
Every woman a miracle,
every child a work in progress.

The Invincible Woman goes viral

You're walking downtown, thinking maybe you do miss the costume, the stupid code name, the old headquarters-turned-Bank of America, when the man bumps into the woman in front of you, and is off with her purse. You give chase, of course. It's easy enough to catch him and pin him against the wall | punch and shatter the bricks by his head because, for once, you want someone to fear you. He pulls a gun, so you palm the muzzle, let the bullet blunt against your skin. By now, everyone is well acquainted with the sound of gunfire and violence, so they run or whip out cell phones to capture the chaos. It's only when you yell for someone to get help that two officers magically appear with guns drawn, yelling at you to drop the poor purse snatcher. You look down. Your hand is still gripped around the muzzle, his around the trigger. The officer's yelling so loud you can't understand a word, so you drop the man and the gun, and when you turn and raise your hands up, one cop opens fire anyway. The other just watches as two bullets ricochet off your skin and strike his partner in his heart, his head. He's dead before he hits the ground, before the crowd stops recording you lowering your hands.

Doctor Freeman

Give enough time
and all things heroic
turn barbaric. How
does a Kansas
housewife rate
against history?
We don't call it
lobotomy anymore,
but we can isolate
the part of the brain
that controls those
dangerous gifts.
78 percent success rate
and you're welcomed
back into humanity.
Viola! No more
exploding hands,
no more telepathy,
no more
invincible women.

you're watching tv in your own home

when the police arrive on your doorstep to inform you that your body is a dangerous weapon, and do you have a license for your body? You blink. They present you with handcuffs, which the arresting officer assures is a courtesy, so please be kind enough to avoid a scene. You remind them you're standing in your own home, and didn't you save their world once, a hundred, a million times over? They blink, don't recall, which doesn't surprise you: you're invisible when well behaved. You notice four officers with guns drawn standing right outside. They'll never learn, never change. Your neighbors are on their porches watching everything go down. *Please*, the arresting officer says, and it's the plea that infuriates you. You try not to recall all the times someone like you has pleaded to someone like them, and what always follows in churches, streets, parks, pulled-over cars, the side of the road, grocery stores, your own neighborhood, your own home, your own country, if any hero, any officer, any American deems it so.

the handcuffs

~

don't feel like anything around your wrists. That's how you know you've turned it off—your ability to feel. It's involuntary sometimes, though you've been practicing for years: you'd touch your own shoulders or make small dimples into your underarm flesh, closing your eyes until you could register the smallest sensation of your own fingers. You were raised to be invincible, to shrug off pain. It's a myth you can't break. But goddamn, can't you just enjoy the taste of a good drink? An orgasm? After years of practice, you found yourself able to enjoy buttery pastries, another person's tongue. Sometimes during fights, you let a little pain get through to remind yourself it's better to just get the fuck outta the way rather than take every blow just because you can.

~

When the entire squad car rises into the air, the officers in the front panic, and you would too, but you already know who it is and can't help but roll your eyes when the car hits the ground with the lightest of touches. The officers are shaken but unharmed, so you push and roll out of the car, tearing the side door off the frame as easily as you snap the cuffs, just in time to witness the other two squad cars stack neatly on top of the one you just escaped, the side door reattaching itself to the car. *Cutting it close, _____*, he says, standing in the middle of the road, grinning, even though it's all *bullshit, I could've gotten out on my own*. You brush the dust off your clothes and before you know it, he's hugging you, and you embrace him for a moment, not knowing what else to do, and you can feel his unshaved cheek against your neck, which nearly brings you to tears. The half dozen cops trapped in their cars are screaming and yelling and threatening to open fire, but you both know they'll only hurt themselves. It's the only thing they know how to do.

The Invincible Woman reunites with The Telepath

~

You admit to yourself that the years have been a little kinder to you than to her, and of course, since she's a telepath, she hears what you think and gives you one of those *well fuck you too* looks, and because you aren't a telepath, you can't tell if it's a tease or sincere. The crime fighting and years of operating on little sleep, the stares, the constant reassurance that you were one of the good ones: you want to believe you put all this behind you, but when The Telepath tells you about the children enslaved inside the artificial moons, you already know what you'll do, how you'll respond, even if it sounds as farfetched as defeating a rogue sun in a series of escalating riddles (long story). It's when The Telepath lets you touch a young girl's mind who's only known bondage and light that you begin to weep, wondering if humans will ever be worth a goddamn. And knowing the answer. *There are thousands*, The Telepath says. *Our people need our help*. Our people. You want to ask what she means, but you know. And The Telepath being a telepath, she knows you know it too.

~

You arrive with banana bread and coffee for everyone when The Telepath lets you in. She jokes that you read her mind, and you both chuckle. If it hurt to see her earlier, it hurts more to see her now in a home you don't recognize with a few people already sitting in the living room, broadcasting you weren't the first she reached out to. She leads you into the kitchen where The Willpower Man is already pulling out a bread knife, mugs, and plates. The three of you catch up on small talk (spilling the tea on all the old and not-so-old teammates who quit, died, disappeared) before you finally ask her what the plan is and she suggests you suit back up and do a few acts of kindness to get the public back on your side before you get down to the real business of taking down moons. *We're not alone*, she says.

The Invincible Woman learns to fly

Tonight we have to knock a child-powered moon from the sky. It's not unlike most nights when we were younger, always facing off against narcissistic gods, evil mutants and neo-Nazis out to kill us every night. But shit ain't changed. You raise your arms like that's really doing something, and I think back to when we were children and I first lifted you a foot above the gym floor. Seeing you float made me drop you on your back. You laughed and asked, *Can we try again?* I was afraid I might fuck up and hurt you and you chided, *You can't hurt me, remember?* I felt awful, thinking about everything you went through to know that, while I practiced floating basketballs in midair in my beat-up K-Swiss. Tonight, I slowly raise you into the sky, then faster, and soon you're rocketing through the night: a miracle of a woman turned star. I'm earthbound and watching when you impact the moon's surface. You crack it open like an egg, let slip the yolk of children, and ride it back to earth. I've caught a hundred boys and girls by the time I find you standing on top of the cratered body, your face freckled with cosmic dust, a shit-eating grin, *Again.*

newscast

We didn't mean to hurt you, Lennon or Hathaway once sang. On the evening news, another moon crashes into the Hudson. They showed the culprits and we couldn't believe it, but we were not surprised. Still, it hurt to see them tearing the moon open and spilling its guts. Conspiracy theories abound about our moons—children batteries, black hole engines, a gift from an alien empire, but we knew it for what is was: justification for radicalism, extremism, treason. Our ex-saviors turned terrorists, determined to plunge us back into night. We didn't want to believe they would hurt us, but here they were, darkening the sky.

The Invincible Woman and The Willpower Man make a comeback

You hold out your cigarette for a friend who's not there, then quickly retract your forgetful arm. I notice, but say nothing, too busy tugging at my collar, grabbing my stomach with both hands and wondering, *Have I always been this fat?* You crack a smile. Eye me up and down, and shake your head. There are men on fire. Men falling from the sky. Men almost upon us. *Almost time*, I tell you as you put out your cigarette; the children are just now waking up. You remind me that I can stop holding my breath. *It's fine*, you say. The people come at us with their cameras and light—each of them asking a different question, all of them wanting the same answer: *Where have you been? Where did you go? Are you here to stay? Why do you hate us? Aren't you afraid?*

acts of kindness

It is endless. Saving children from moons, saving your people and their people from the parade of killers. You block bullets with your body, disarm the culprit, refrain from killing him, though he deserves it. No, he deserves worse. But you're not capable of deliverance. The congregation prays for the victim and the shooter alike, survivors offer forgiveness and grace and you're taught this is the proper way to suffer. Your country is full of noble victims and corrupt leaders and misguided youths and radical extremists and domestic terrorists and everyone begins to bleed into the same American. You worry that your presence escalates violence, you worry more that your absence would yield greater disasters. How different would the world be without you? You disconnect each child from their compartment, too young to understand what their country is doing to them under the small lights of indifferent stars.

The Invincible Woman attends a meeting

Your people are dying and together you can save them if you can all stop shouting for just a goddamn minute. Everyone surrounds the table covered with blueprints of moons. You stand in the back and watch without saying a word. Someone says it's past time something more was done. Knocking out moons isn't enough; look what happened to the last group they celebrated. You wince at this mention, thankful that only a few eyes turn to you. Someone else asks what are you going to do with the people that did this to us? Tempers flare and The Telepath quiets everyone down. You step outside and light a cigarette on the front porch, watch the clouds, and wait for your marching orders. A man is burning dead leaves by simply placing his hands over the pile, a woman walks her dog by the house and waves. You wave hello and blow smoke towards the silent sky when you catch the glint of the drone and realize it's too late to do anything but survive.

The Never-Ending Man

I'm used to cracked bones
fusing back to spine: mementos

of what's been done to me
& mine. My body a blackboard

the world chalks up. You want
to know how I feel? I prefer felt

erasers over pink, the black
brush over hard rubber. I jump

off the tallest building,
go splat. Get scraped clean

the next day.
Oh, how wonderful!

To die every night!
To always come back to life.

I've so many lives, I've filled
the Atlantic, every unmarked grave

adorned with seashells & stone—
cold water & dry land,

my country knows
how to say hello.

I grin and bear it,
my teeth harder than my tender

skull, I chew
before swallowing

every good lie: this'll be
the last time, you

can do anything, watch me
fly.

The Invincible Girl

They asked you what you wanted to be called. By then they had tried to drown you, lit you on fire, strapped bombs to your body, strapped your body to a wall, and shot you with every weapon they could find. They suspected what you already knew: nothing could kill you. *The Invincible Woman*, you said. They said, *How about Girl?* You told them if you were old enough to be killed, you were old enough to name yourself. *But we can't kill you*, they said. And you asked who earns the right to name survival? They introduced you to the other children as *The Invincible Woman*. One boy raised his hand. *I want to change my name*, he said. The boy nodded at you, you nodded back.

move

after Lucille Clifton

There are think pieces on *what brought us here*, and you're never included in *us*. Everywhere people can talk, they talk: you had it coming. Soon. Numbers tickertape the bottom of the screen. There are interviews with neighbors a few blocks over that felt the heat but were otherwise unscathed. When is a bomb not a bomb? When it's a preemptive strike. What is the proper response to your country? You have some ideas: some are full of forgiveness and grace—all kindness and tenderness till it rubs you raw, but you'd like to abandon mercy altogether. On television a young girl calls on the audience to vote for her, so she's not sent home. They're already planning to launch another moon into the sky. You want to try everything on, see what fits best.

Goliath

We prop the body up
but it blocks the sky.

If we lay it down, we'd have
to uproot too many trees,

and we cannot leave him
in the sun, in the dark. There is a hole

through his chest—the light
finds a way to bend

through him. We could bury
the body, but who can afford

to buy enough plots,
and how many plots will it take?

Eighty? Two hundred?
Who will dig the graves? Who

will call the men & machines
to chew enough earth?

Enough with the body, please
give him a name.

—Goliath.

But we already have
a Goliath: the one who steps

over buildings, cups men
& women in the prison

of his palms.
Choose another.

—Black Goliath?

Yes. Ok. We
could disassemble Black

Goliath, cut him to pieces,
blow him to atoms.

We could use rope
or chains to drag him

to the river, or wrench
him apart with steel.

Rope would not hold him.
He would leave grooves too deep

to drag. And no one wants
a body raining from the sky.

Then we leave him
to lie in the sun.

There will still be bones.

But bones we can use.
Bones we can unearth

and polish years from now—
build a playground

for children, let them swing freely
from his ivory ribs.

moon

~

You bring the last moon down on a Tuesday. The sun is out. The Willpower Man chews his tongue as the crowd, marching towards you, shakes in fear like a shimmering white mirage. You know what's coming and foolishly believe what's coming can't hurt you.

~

The Telepath and The Willpower Man are helping the children who have spilled out of the cracked moon, calming them down, freeing them from the mess of cables and wires. You stand in front, prepared to greet the crowd. They stop when they're close enough to see you and to see what's happening behind you. *That moon was ours*, they say, ignoring the children behind you. *You've ruined everything*, they say, ignoring the moon still orbiting the world. What could you say to stop these people who are already reaching for their guns. *Think about what you're doing*, you say, realizing it won't be enough.

~

The people level their rifles at you. The people pull out knives and axes and sharp sticks. They will fail to kill you, but you cannot protect everyone, and once the killing starts you fear what you'll do. *Fear.* You want to laugh: after all this time, you now fear yourself. Ain't that something?

~

The Telepath's nose begins to bleed, and everyone stops what they're doing and lowers their weapons and blink in unison. Some of them begin to weep. Others vomit. You, too, feel the familiar pull of The Telepath like an itch on the back of your skull, and subsequently feel the people crowd around the borders of your consciousness. You're touching everyone's wet hearts, and you're all so vulnerable and afraid and she tells you *everything is going to be ok*, and you believe her. You lie down on a soft bed that stretches from horizon to horizon, surrounded by other soft bodies under a perfect sun shining perfect light in perfect weather. You turn around to ask what she's done, but only catch the light of the dying moon shine through a small hole in The Telepath's chest. The second bullet bounces off your cheek as you turn to catch her as she falls towards you.

~

Surprisingly, no one else fires. The crowd is still in a euphoric stupor (except for, at least, one person). Impossible to know who pulled the trigger. You feel helpless for only the fourth time in your life, holding your friend who is already gone. You look down at her blank face and immediately regret it; you try not to erupt. The people are beginning to wake up, but you keep your back to them and instead look at The Willpower Man and he looks right back, eager to act. You give him the smallest of nods. His face cracks into a laugh. He looks at the crowd. And every fear floods right back inside everyone.

necropolis

> Trust me. Death is just a different kind of journey to the land that I am king of.
>
> —T'Challa

Call me King of two worlds:
the endless sun and the hearts

of my people which only beat
because somewhere, someone

created us this way: call it Bast
or Lee, I was born

silhouetted by a sun, raised between
the word and the act:

an object to be hurled against
heroes hunkered below:

I was created to please:
rendered above Kirbyesque machines,

shadowed by every face I've lost:
they smile before they turn

and walk into the sun. Father,
why must I live in the shade?

Let me give this crown away: let
me go with my people, walk them

home, back to the black heart:
let me send off every last one.

The Heartless Boy

He lent his eyes to his sister so she could carry them in her pocket as she climbed their backyard oak. He was afraid of heights but stood below, blind and waiting. She perched on the heaviest branch and lifted his eyes so he could see the horizon's rim before dropping one eye, which made the boy afraid of the world suddenly rushing upwards—his own small body below, his desperate open hands. He kept to himself for years after that. Until high school, until he left his hands with his tutor to practice scales while he went to parties where girls poured drinks down his throat, his face flushed red. He loaned himself out more: for money, junior classmen would hide his chest under their jackets and let it take the bully's blows; for pleasure, he'd mail his tongue cross-country to taste all sorts of food—Hatch green chile in the fall, fresh smoked oysters in the south. When he first told his parents, his mother cried, his father's rage eclipsed his fear. To calm them down, he gave each one part of his heart and assured them if they kept it safe, he would live forever. His father quieted, amazed his son could do such things, would sometimes ask him to remove his ear as a parlor trick or have him stand in another room and tell the difference between a pilsner and a pale ale while they submerged his tongue in two different pints. *Incredible* and *what a waste of beer*, the drunk men would say, but to their credit, they kept it secret and only told their families, their coworkers, their neighbors' wives when afterwards, to appease their guilt, they would lie and imagine the disembodied tongue or nose or eye—how every part of the body wants to feel useful. Needed. His mother never fell for tricks, but understood her husband's awe, her son's eagerness to please. Still, it terrified her to see her son in powder blue and white tights, a thin face mask—*The Heartless Boy* fighting crime, getting shot where his heart should be. A name the boy grew to hate the older he got. But the world insisted that would forever be his name. He lost track of the years, he felt foolish eating mussels he couldn't taste, and he realized he had forgotten his dead mother's face. His father's and his sister's too, and he forgot what they borrowed, what he had freely given away. He decided to quit so he could dedicate more time to finding himself but disappeared instead. Though sometimes at parties, people swore they had witnessed the most miraculous thing: a man who could pluck out his own eyes and still tell you what he saw. Plunge a chef's knife through his chest and not wince from the pain.

IV

The Invincible Woman becomes god

~

You stood in front of a star larger than the sun. It wasn't actually a star because it could talk and you could hear its voice even though it had no mouth and it moved like pure light if pure light were a small child trying to gain purchase on a stool that was too tall. But if someone asked you what it looked like, the closest thing you could think to say was *star*.

~

So you were facing the star and it told you that it had come to destroy the Earth. You asked why, and it replied that the Earth did not deserve to live. You demanded to know why. It told you that it was a star and it was powerful and you were nothing and the Earth was nothing, so why did it need a reason? Did you give a reason every time you swatted one gnat but not another? You suddenly felt hot and looked around and couldn't see the Earth, which was probably a relief, because if you could see the Earth from where you were, that probably meant it was already too late. But you couldn't see anything but the star and Blackness, and you were not afraid, in fact you were comforted, and the star sensed this and issued a challenge: it would spare the Earth if you could hide it for a day. You said that was unfair. Impossible. The star reminded you that you dealt in impossibility every day.

~

When you opened your eyes, you were back on Earth and the star was nowhere to be found. You did not feel safe and knew that by tomorrow the world would be destroyed. You didn't tell anyone for a time because it seemed unfair to tell someone the world was over and none of you could do anything about it, so you took a smoke break with your teammates and said nothing until a stray thought entered your mind.

~

One of your teammates could open doors through space and step through, perfect for catching fall victims or bar hopping across the world in a single night. All he needed was to see the other side, which was easy since your other teammate was a telepath who could peak into anyone's mind and could share what they saw and within a few seconds ∧ you could all be there too. You called your teammate *Doorman*—a name he hated: it was reductive and telegraphed his gifts. You told him your name had the same issues, but you just leaned into it, and he should stop being a bitch about it and do the same. *Ouch*, he said, then you both laughed and fell into an easy friendship.

~

But could your teammate open a door big enough for the world to fit through? He never tried it before, so maybe? But where to hide the world? Where is a place no one, or star, could see? You had an idea. When you were young, before you realized you were gifted, you daydreamed about the safe and kind world. Couldn't your teammate hide the world within that fantasy?

~

Impossible, Doorman said. The Telepath disagreed and peered into your mind and shared one of your old memories. *Open the door here*, she said. *But*, he argued, *no one can hold eight billion minds or people, or much less the physical planet.* The Telepath hesitated, then volunteered one of her memories instead, but you all knew she couldn't do it—if she possessed more than a few dozen people at once, she'd get a nosebleed. *It won't kill me*, you argued. *Nothing can.* Of course, you didn't know this for sure.

~

The Telepath put you to sleep and guided Doorman through your earliest and fondest memories until he found the perfect spot: he waited until night to make the doorway as big as the Earth, and it cleanly passed through the door and fell into perfect orbit around the imaginary perfect sun of your imaginary perfect world. If people were afraid, they didn't show it. Or you probably just slept through their panic. Either way, you were thankful for sleep, otherwise you would have worried about how you could exist outside/inside your own mind simultaneously—although didn't everyone exist outside and inside their own mind? And walked and talked with other people holding different versions of themselves inside? Wasn't this what we had always done?

~

When you finally did wake up, you were floating alone in space—no Earth, only the moon spinning off into the galaxy and the rogue star barreling towards you. *Impressive*, the star said. It was furious and vowed you had made a lifelong enemy and one day at the end of both of your long lives, you would see each other again. Then it left.

~

You closed your eyes again, until you felt The Telepath's touch from inside your mind and opened your eyes and a doorway appeared, and the Earth came back through the planet-sized door. And before it could fly too far off, you pointed at the moon spinning through space, and another doorway appeared in the distance and caught the flying moon and placed it back in orbit around the Earth.

~

There were later adjustments to make to ensure the Earth and moon were exactly where they originally belonged. The Willpower Man helped wrangle it in place, and soon someone had the idea that since the moon had nearly run away, why not create a backup moon just in case? And that idea grew into more and more moons—problems for another time. And when people retold the story, they changed important details, as did you, and sometimes you were left out entirely, and most people just believed it was fiction, forgetting it was true. But once you held the entire world and did not break. All eight billion lives tucked inside you, protected and safe.

EPILOGUE

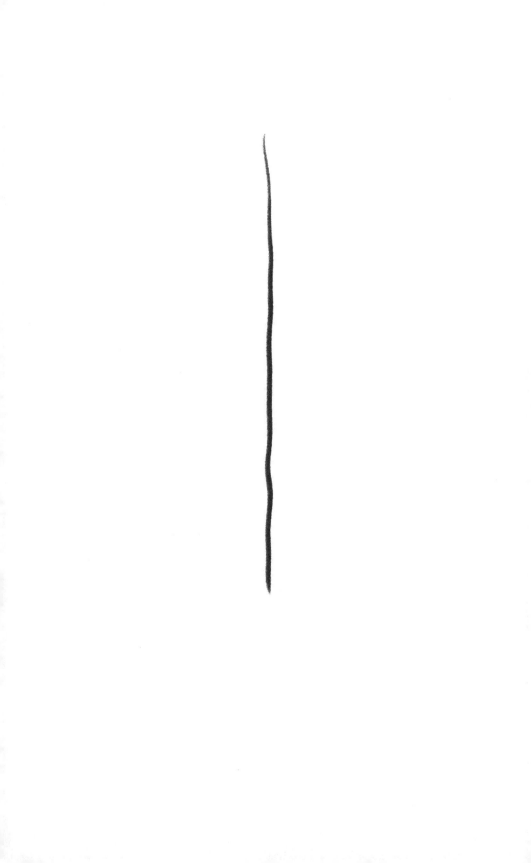

small lives

You wake from burning in a field with little urgency—even in dream the heat can't touch you. But when you open your eyes, you kick off the sheets, touch the bare thigh pressed against your skin, but they're deep in sweeter dreams. You could've saved your friend from the gun, from the rope. Could've snatched the bullet from air with your bare hand. But you've never been fast. Just strong. When the fires come, the fires come. When morning comes, you're dead tired, brew coffee, no breakfast, head to your morning shift where the tips are decent and the regulars are quiet drunks who ask you by name for another beer and nod in thanks, give you small and constant offerings: dirty dollar bills, handful of coins, sometimes a treat—tin of cookies their adult children dropped off for the holiday, so sweet you swear you can taste every grain of sugar. Your favorite.

Bruce's Beach

I saw you on tv yesterday, selling life insurance in an old commercial. Elbowed the man next to me and said, *I once threw her to the moon.* He didn't believe me and only asked, *Which one?*

All of them, I told him, *until there was only one left.* He blinked. Maybe he forgot we were back down to just one. Maybe he didn't like that I had taken something from him, or he was too drunk to give a damn about any of it. But then he said one of the moons was named after his father, and so was he. *You must be proud*, I said, which he took seriously and told me he was awarded a university scholarship, a good job, and a low-interest loan all based—he assumed—on being named after a moon. *It brought me good luck*, he said. Then he paid my tab and wished some of that luck on me.

overdue

When you place them on the counter, the librarian's eyes don't follow the small stack of books but instead rise to your face. She stammers recognition: *You, you, you…!* surprised at her own excitement. You smile and take one step back, expecting to be done with this transaction when the librarian grabs an old index card. *Could you sign something for us?* You grab the nearby pen and oblige with something inspirational and benign. The librarian does a little clap, *Oh thank you so much! We really appreciate it.* Honestly, people are so cute—always saying *we* and *us*! How often they slip into collectives, become nations unto themselves. When was the last time you referred to yourself as a people? Thought of yourself as community? If you did, who knows, maybe there'd be more of you left.

origin story

If I could take it back, trust that I would.
I believe you when you tell me
to go back where I came from. Oh,
if I could. But I came from you, so let's not
be mad that I'm always greeted by
the murderers, the animal lovers
who treat us like animals, the rally
full of men demanding their country
back. Let's start over—do right
by me & I'll leave you alone. All I want
is a little peace. Otherwise, I'm trouble
you can't shake. Every day you say it's
us or you. Don't worry, I know exactly
what you mean. America, I mean
to be your first and second plane.

The Invincible Woman has a one-night stand

You pour whiskey too heavy, drafts with too much head. Heft kegs as if they were stacks of cocktail napkins and stop a bar fight by placing yourself between two men—the bottle shattering against your body and everyone too drunk to notice there's no blood, just spilt domestic beer. Over break, you bum a cigarette from a woman who says you once saved her life a lifetime ago. You want to deny it, but you'll take what gratefulness you can get. She blows smoke in your face, her breath full of sweetness you wish you could touch. Afterwards, she's fast asleep under low-thread-count sheets you can't feel, but you can tell. You're craving a smoke so you throw on your jeans and shirt and step out on her front porch. By the time she wakes and joins you outside, you tell her you both know you were never the woman who saved her from disaster. She calls it simple confusion between one miracle and another. You call it a good line. She laughs and wonders if you ever dream about donning that tight costume again, already plotting her next fantasy. You'll wear it for her someday, you lie. She touches your arm, marvels at your skin, how the years haven't worn you down. You joke all the violence just sandpapered you smooth.

on corrective thinking

At the rally, after locking every man in place, I ask each one the same question: *What would you do if our positions were reversed?* They each think the same answer, so I make a fist, make their bodies crack like ice when it hits hot water. The men still waiting their turn slowly begin to understand. Too late.

osteology

~

The point of the class exercise is to identify and categorize the bones. First: cause of death, which is easy—the bones are bare in the way only fire can clean. Microscopic observation dates them no older than seventeen, both female. And then the real fun: chemical analysis to map their DNA, despite degradation, enough left to cross list with a database to determine ancestry and any potential gifts. Scrape a large enough sample and maybe it can be preserved, replicated, and perfected. Their deaths will not be in vain, they will pass on their gifts and strong genes.

~

The professor has been a good company man for over thirty years, but when he looks over the bones he feels a twinge of hate towards his students, towards the countless young faces who will eventually benefit from this research that will never know the names of these bones who will never know rest. The professor thinks they need a proper burial, at least, and argues as much in department meetings, on the floor of the faculty senate, emails to the president, but they compromise: let's put them on display instead! Celebrate them! We know how to properly honor ~~their~~ our dead.

~

The professor knows he'll be fired, tenured or no, driving across state lines with two skeletons packed in a trunk. He doesn't even know who to give the bones to or where he's going; there are no living relatives anyone has ~~cared~~ been able to find. Still, the professor finds himself in a neighborhood in Philadelphia, PA where there's now a ridiculously small park tucked between two houses that may have once been their family home. Before he can grab the shovel from the trunk, a man touches down from the sky and frightens the professor at first. He has a face the professor can almost recall, but he only sees the face of his dead brother when he looks at him, which can't be right. He's confused and afraid, and the man simply places his hand on the professor's shoulder and tells him to go home. The professor nervously gets back in the car and drives for a while before pulling over and falling asleep. When he wakes up the next morning, he finds the trunk is empty, and the bones and the man who wasn't his dead brother are gone.

fly

Still dark. My baby girl leaps
out the window to greet
the rising sun. I stand below
ready to catch her, but every time
she takes off without fail,
her laughter calling to the orioles,
calling to my shame
that had I the choice, I would have never
taught her to fly.

Somewhere there is a man
with a gun
who will take pleasure
in seeing her skin
against the pure blue sky—
and shooting her down.
My own mother did not flinch
when I first raised my arms
and lifted my feet off the ground,
above her head. She only said,
*You better hope bulletproof skin
comes with that gift.* Years later
I found out it did.

the new world

you closed your eyes last night
believing this world would be yours
forever. That was your dream. And like mine,
it was a lie . . . here is a new truth:
while you slept, the world changed.

—Charles Francis Xavier

Casings and screams hit concrete. The snow's falling so fast it buries every thought and prayer the politicians will deliver on *Meet the Press* next week. But now the candy canes deflate, and people run through the dead evergreens due for a price reduction. You were about to ask the salesman for a fresh cut when four bullets strike you and the salesman falls over, slipping on the slush. He checks his body and looks at you as if you're already dead. You grab one of the bullets that hit you—blunted and spent on the ground. *Oh my god jesus lord christ almighty jesus lord christ oh jesus oh jesus oh jesus* the salesman scrambles to his feet. Watching him run, the old part of you rises to the surface. You turn towards the gunfire. The shooter's not moving very fast or far, just taking steps through the trees and firing, and when he sees you walking towards him, he pauses—unsure how to respond. The old lessons come back: make yourself an easy target, bait their need for violence with your body. It works. He fires off several rounds, and it takes a moment for him to realize that nothing is stopping you. He's too young to remember you or yours. He only knows men who launch rockets instead of moons and try to make any lie true through willful ignorance alone. Someone once said, *You must not remind them that giants walk the earth*; your hand fused around the killer's jaw, his eyes blazing with newfound fear, say otherwise.

work

The boy bought a candy bar, a soda, surgical masks, and a two-pack of Swisher Sweets. He walked home in the Georgia heat and drank his coke in one long swallow, wary of every headlight. At home, he found his mother sleeping, but checked her breath to make sure, remembering stories of how she did the same for him when he was a baby. Now she checked his clothes for drugs or blood and thanked God every day for never finding either. She prayed for scholarships and job offers, dismissing moments of doubt to the devil's work. The boy knew she meant well but chances were he'd never leave town unless he had to, and though his mother told him no one lived small lives, he couldn't help but feel some lives were large enough to see from outer space. And those lives mattered more. But if this was his life, he didn't mind it. The boy went to his room, locked the door, and jumped out the window and rode the air all the way to Savannah. He sat on the rooftop of a hotel until he was good and faded, watching people below like a hawk, letting the breeze blow through his hoodie. This was work. Work he'd have until it killed him. He didn't mind. He thought of his mother working backbreaking days and backbreaking nights at the post office, lifting boxes alongside her sister (who got her the job), and how one night her legs gave out and she said she couldn't take it. Her sister kicked her and hissed, *Get up! Get your ass up or we'll both be out of here!* How she picked herself up without complaint or falling again, she never said, but the boy could guess. Same reason he was perched on the rooftop's ledge, his hood flipped up, the strings pulled tight around his neck. He blew smoke, his eyes alert, then stooped on the man exiting the bar below. The man screamed until he couldn't, until velocity forced his mouth shut. The pale moon lit his pale face. He passed out from the sudden shift in altitude and fear. The man never came to, not even when the boy dropped him off in a small clearance about twenty miles south. The earth was so wet, the boy felt if he stayed on the ground too long it'd swallow him whole. Two women waited nearby, one gave the boy an envelope with money and the boy nodded in thanks. The woman didn't smile at what little of his face she saw but allowed herself a small moment of joy watching him fly off and tapped her sister on the shoulder to ask, *Ever see such a thing?* Her sister shook her head, then pulled out her knife, turned her attention to the man, and together they got to work.

small lives

Acknowledgments

Grateful acknowledgement is made to the editors of the following publications, where the following poems originally appeared, some in different forms and with different titles:

Academy of American Poets: Poem-A-Day: "fly"
Bellingham Review: "population boom"
Columbia Journal: "The Invincible Woman reunites with The Telepath," "The Invincible Woman and The Willpower Man make a comeback," and "The Invincible Woman has a one-night stand"
Copper Nickel: "The Telepath quits her day job," "The Willpower Man," and "work"
Drawn to Marvel: Poems from the Comic Books, edited by Bryan D. Dietrich and Marta Ferguson: "old lions"
Dreaming Awake: New Contemporary Prose Poetry from the United States, Australia, and England, edited by Peter Johnson and Cassandra Atherton: "comic book plots & origin stories," "The Invincible Woman makes the front page," "The Telepath listens to the flowers and the trees," and "The Telepath finds the bright side"
Ice On a Hot Stove: A Decade of Converse MFA Poetry, edited by Denise Duhamel and Rick Mulkey: "fiat lux"
Indiana Review: "Goliath"
Inscape: "overdue"

The Laurel Review: "origin story"

Motionpoems: "tryouts" (animated poem)

Multiverse! An Anthology of Superhero Poetry of Superhuman Proportions, edited by Rob Sturma and Ryk Mcintyre: "Astro Boy blues"

Solstice: A Magazine of Diverse Voices: "The Invincible Woman goes viral"

Transition: The Magazine of Africa and the Diaspora: "tryouts"

Waxwing Literary Journal: "The Invincible Woman enjoys her night off"

The Weekly Hubris: "men on fire," "▇▇▇▇▇▇ History Month," and "you're watching tv in your own home"

West Branch: "The Invincible Woman goes to a party," "The Never-Ending Man," and "small lives"

This book wouldn't be possible without the guidance, patience, support, camaraderie, and innumerable insights from too many people to list fully here, but special gratitude goes out to Kyle Churney, Mari Crabtree, Amy Fleury, Yona Harvey, Jonathan Bohr Heinen, Esther Lee, Juan Morales, Rick Mulkey, Oliver de la Paz, Marianna Vick, and everyone who has endured years of my comic-book-obsessed poems.

Special thanks to the 2022 Art Omi Writers Residency crew, including Ruth Adams, Maria Adelmann, Elisa Wouk Almino, Chiara Baffa, T. J. Benson, Marcia Burnier, DW Gibson, Catherine Lacey, Susana Moreira Marques, Ucheoma Onwutuebe, Rita Soares-Kern, Sebastian Stuertz, Natalia Trigo, and Miquael Williams, for the wonderful company and enriching conversations and providing such a necessary space for developing these poems.

Another heartfelt shout-out to my guiding stars Elise McHugh and Hilda Raz as well as the crew at the University of New Mexico Press for believing in this book.

For Conseula Francis, who would've loved this.

For my mother, Kim, for introducing me to comics and sharing that lifelong love. And for that nine-year-old boy who first fell into the pages of *The Incredible Hulk*, no. 372, and never looked back.

And as always, for Lisa, for everything.

Notes

The opening epigraphs are from the poems "1933" by Lynda Hull, originally published in *Ghost Money* (1986), and from "note, passed to superman" by Lucille Clifton, originally published in *The Book of Light* (1993).

"rehearsal" is partially inspired by states, including South Carolina, that can still institute the death penalty by firing squad.

"The Telepath follows the bad man" references the January 17, 1989, school shooting at Cleveland Elementary School in Stockton, California.

"The Invincible Woman enjoys her night off" includes lyrics from "Love Hangover" by Diana Ross from her 1976 album *Diana Ross*.

"tales to astonish" shares the name of a Marvel Comics series *Tales to Astonish* that originally ran from 1959 to 1968.

The title of "no more water" is an excerpt from the passage "God gave Noah the rainbow sign. No more water, the fire next time!" from James Baldwin's 1963 book *The Fire Next Time*.

The opening lines of "a different world" are borrowed from Jake Chambers: a character in Stephen King's 1982 book *The Gunslinger*. The phrase "brutal imagination" is a nod towards Cornelius Eady's 2001 book *Brutal Imagination*.

All characters in "old lions" are Black comic book characters from Marvel Comics, DC Comics, and Dell Comics. For further context, Prince Waku first appeared in *Jungle Tales*, vol. 1, by Don Rico and Ogden Whitney, published by Atlas Comics (soon to be Marvel) in 1954. Lobo first appeared in *Lobo* by Don D. J. Arneson and Tony Tallarico, published by Dell Comics in 1965, and has the distinction of being the first African American hero to star in his own comic book. It was cancelled after two issues.

The first epigraph to "tryouts" is from Audre Lorde's "A Litany for Survival," published in her 1978 collection *The Black Unicorn*. The last line of the poem also borrows the last line from Lorde's poem. The second epigraph is borrowed from the cover of *Justice League of America*, no. 173, by Gerry Conway and Dick Dillin, published in 1979.

The title of "*Welcome to The Amazing, Invincible Woman! Hope you survive the experience!*" is a riff on the semi-famous X-Men phrase that originated on the cover of *The Uncanny X-Men*, no. 139, by Chris Claremont and John Byrne, published in 1980.

The title of "in blackest day, in brightest night" is an inversion of the official oath taken by The Green Lantern Corps.

"Astro Boy blues" references the popular character who first appeared in *Shōnen* magazine in 1952 and was created by Osamu Tezuka.

"Beast Boy" is a reimagining of the DC Superhero Beast Boy, who first appeared in *Doom Patrol*, no. 99, by Arnold Drake and Bob Brown in 1965.

Lines in "the new rules" riff and expand upon various United States Black Codes.

"Doctor Freeman" is a reimagining of Walter Jackson Freeman II, a neurologist who introduced prefrontal lobotomies to the United States (a continuation of work by neurologist António Egas Moniz, who won the Nobel Prize in Physiology or Medicine in 1949). Freeman first performed the procedure in 1936 on Alice Hood Hammatt from Topeka, Kansas.

"newscast" references the song "Jealous Guy," recorded by John Lennon and featured on his 1971 album *Imagine* and covered by Donny Hathaway in 1972.

"The Invincible Woman attends a meeting" and "move" are both informed by the 1985 bombing of 6221 Osage Avenue in Philadelphia, Pennsylvania—an event directly addressed in Lucille Clifton's poem "move," which was published in her 1993 collection *The Book of Light*.

"Goliath" references the comic *Civil War*, no. 4, by Mark Millar and Steve McNiven, published in 2006.

The epigraph to "necropolis" is from the comic *Secret Wars*, no. 7, by Jonathan Hickman and Esad Ribic, published in 2015, and references Black Panther's first appearance on the cover of *Fantastic Four*, no. 52, which was published in 1966.

The title of "Bruce's Beach" refers to a California property purchased by Willa and Charles Bruce in 1912 during the Great Migration and opened as a resort to Black families. In 1924, local city officials condemned and seized the land through eminent domain laws. Ninety-eight years later, the land was finally granted back to the descendants of the Bruce family.

The epigraph to "the new world" is from the comic *House of X*, no. 6, by Jonathan Hickman and Pepe Larraz, published in 2019. The italicized line towards the end is from the comic *The Dark Knight Returns*, no. 3, by Frank Miller, published in 1986.

"work" is partially based on a true story.

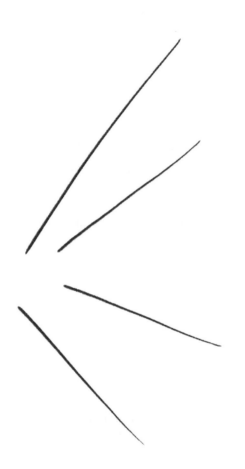

small lives